the Gift of Saint Francis

JOHN DAVIS AND DON MCMONIGLE
ILLUSTRATED BY LYNNE MUIR

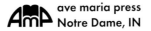

ave maria press
Notre Dame, IN

Published in the U.S.A. by Ave Maria Press, Notre Dame, Indiana, 46556

International Standard Book Number: 0-87793 603-X

www.avemariapress.com

Text: Copyright © 2003 John Davis and Don McMonigle
Illustrations and design: Copyright © 2003 Lynne Muir

First published in Australia by John Garratt Publishing

Typesetting: JamesGrechDesign
Printed by Tien Wah Press, Singapore

Translations of 'The Canticle of the Sun' and 'The Rule' are taken from *Saint Francis of Assisi* by Lawrence Cunningham and photographs by Dennis Stock. Photographs copyright © 1981 by Dennis Stock. Text copyright © 1981 Lawrence Cunningham. Other photographs copyright © 1981 by Scala Communications, Inc. Reprinted by permission of Harper Collins Publishers Inc.

CONTENTS

FOREWORD

FRANCIS OF ASSISI WAS AN ICONOCLAST and spiritual revolutionary who helped to pave the way for the birth of a new, more humane sensibility in Europe. Not only did he wrest back from the medieval church the right of the individual to explore more intimately his own spirituality, he made it possible for everyone to believe in the realisation of Christ in themselves. The Stigmata was much more than a miraculous event; it signified the beginning of man's personal suffering in the name of Christ.

Francis made poetry and wandering the touchstone of his life. In his relatively short ministry, he managed to visit France, Spain, Rhodes, Palestine, Egypt, and possibly Cyprus. He rarely remained in one place for very long. His love of troubadour poetry, and the whole tradition of minstrelry with its emphasis on travelling was central to his life. Refusing the lure of possessions, status, profession, family, even nationality, Francis became the embodiment of the free man.

This new book, both in text and in pictures, offers rare and intriguing insights into the man and his time. Readers will be able to formulate for themselves how unique was Francis of Assisi as a religious reformer and mystic. It is hoped also that readers will make an interior journey of their own in the company of both authors and illustrator, pursuing for themselves the mystery of Divinity that Francis espoused.

James Cowan, author *Francis: A Saint's Way*

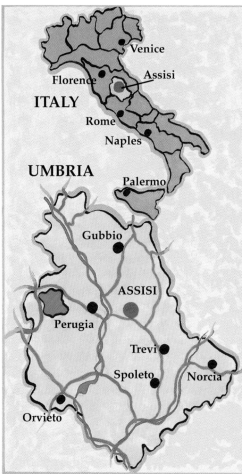

1. Basilica of St Francis

2. Santa Maria Sopra Minerva

3. Santa Chiara

4. Rocca Maggiore (The Castle)

5. The Carceri

6. San Damiano

7. The Portiuncula in
   Santa Maria degli Angeli

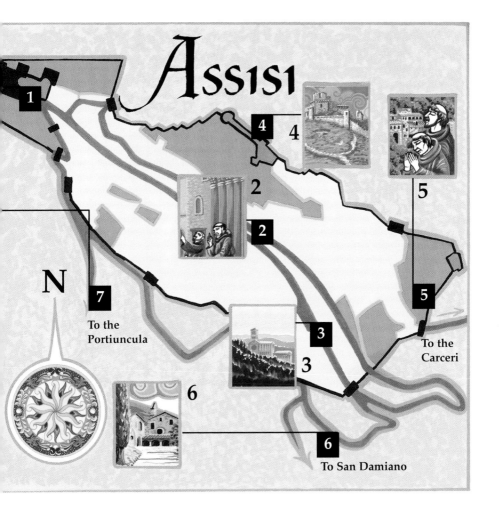

Assisi

1

4
4

2
2

5

5
To the
Carceri

7
To the
Portiuncula

N

3
3

6

6
To San Damiano

OCTOBER 4 MARKS THE FEAST DAY OF ST FRANCIS OF ASSISI, patron saint of Italy. He is the most beloved and generally revered of all the saints of the medieval Church.

Perhaps because of his well-documented love for all God's creatures, he is also considered to be the patron saint for animals. One favourite thirteenth century fresco shows an earnest Francis preaching to an attentive and alert congregation of the birds of the air. They are standing in neat rows, not missing a thing.

The beautiful Umbrian hill town of Assisi is widely recognised as being the home of this great saint of God. The town remains a place of rest and refreshment for countless pilgrims and visitors. The spirit and influence of Francis is never far away.

As visitors we are bowled over by the beauty, by the accumulated faith of the centuries, by the sense of the closeness of God. We look in wonder at the marvellous frescoes, telling the story of Francis. And, if there is enough time, we can explore every nook and cranny of this wonderful place that goes back to Roman times.

So we can stand in the tiny ledge garden at San Damiano's where 'The Canticle of Brother Sun' was written. We can see the window where St Clare held the monstrance aloft in the face of attacking Saracen soldiers. We can climb the very steep road to Francis' hermitage, up on the side of the looming Mount Subasio. We can stride down the cobbled narrow streets of the town in the early morning darkness to the first mass of the day at the saint's tomb, at the very lowest part of the great basilica.

With other pilgrims, we can revel in the simple faithfulness of the hidden Poor Clares, as they joyfully sing their office in their convent church. If you are lucky or well- informed you could be here for a great Assisi occasion, as we were, clinging halfway up an 800-year-old pillar to hear the gospel-fresh words of Mother Teresa. Another saint in another time.

A terrible earthquake hit Assisi in 1997. A lovely place was sorely damaged and torn apart. Lives were lost. Priceless works of art crumbled into nothing – perhaps including those pert rows of

attentive birds. But since then, much has been rebuilt and much has been lovingly restored. Nothing has destroyed the spirit of the place. Francis is still present everywhere.

Pilgrims have never stopped coming to pray, to love and to grow. God is still honoured. Francis, Il Poverello – the little poor one – still brings all those who are open and searching, closer to God.

This book is a small appreciation from two such searchers.

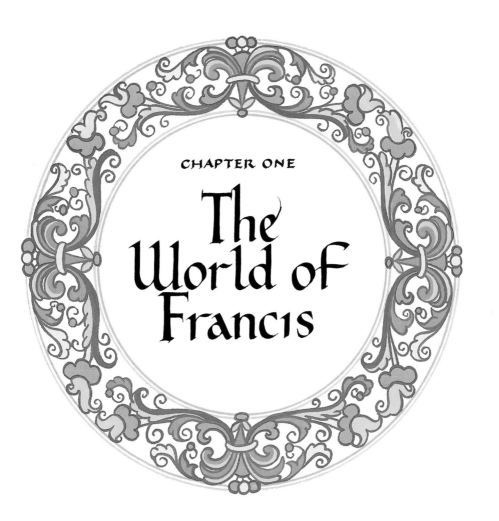

CHAPTER ONE

The World of Francis

THE WORLD OF FRANCIS BERNADONE was that of the late Middle Ages. Often referred to as the Age of Faith, it was a period when the Church was the most powerful force in society. It was an age

that witnessed the construction of the great cathedrals like Notre Dame and Chartres in France, and Durham and Canterbury cathedrals in England. It was the Church that was also responsible for the great learning that marked the age. The huge monastic foundations and medieval universities proved fertile ground for the emergence of the leading intellectuals and Church leaders who still today, are considered among the Church's most brilliant thinkers. St Bernard of Clairvaux, St Anselm and Francis' immediate contemporary, St Dominic, to name a few, contributed much to the age and enjoyed great respect during their lives.

It was Bernard, for instance, with whom we connect yet another significant phenomenon of the period, the Crusades. It was at Vezelay, France on Easter Day, 1146 that Bernard preached at the beginning of the Second Crusade. The Crusades were still a reality

of medieval life sixty years later when Francis made his own visit to the East in 1219.

It was a period of great religious zeal, a zeal that at times led to the fanaticism and popularity of some movements becoming too closely aligned to the masses and the eventual disapproval of the Church. The Cathars, Albigensians and Waldensians, each in their time came to experience such disapproval, suppression and the ultimate charge of heresy.

Another great symbol that dominated medieval life was the castle. In Francis' own town of Assisi the citizens nestled close under the walls of the castle, a symbol of allegiance, power and protection in times of great unrest and danger.

The castle also reminds us of another significant feature of medieval life – courtly love – the courteous yearning of intensely beloved, but separated parties. The French ideas of chivalry and courtly life dominated much of medieval life, expressed through literature as in the enormously popular work of the period, *The*

Romance of the Rose, and poetry such as in Dante's 'Vita Nuova', or the lyrics of the troubadours. It was also a popular subject among artists as seen in many of the paintings and tapestries of the period.

It was also an age marked by significant commerce and trade. Great trade routes crossed the European continent to the East as well as along the great pilgrimage routes. Francis' own father was engaged in such activity as a cloth merchant. In fact, Francis' birth in 1182 occurred on an occasion when his father was away conducting business in France. It was in honour of that country, despite his son being baptised Giovanni, that his father named him Francesco. It was by this name that he was known for the rest of his life.

The
Young
Francis

LIKE MANY OTHER GREAT RELIGIOUS FIGURES before him, Francis Bernadone's early years gave no indication of the extraordinary life that was to follow. The crisis was yet to come. Like Saul, the son of Kish, going out to look for his father's asses, Francis did not know there was to be a point in his life when God would intervene in a most decisive way. This was not to occur until his early twenties.

Raised in one of the typical hill towns in Umbria in central Italy, Francis' childhood and formative years were little different to those experienced by his contemporaries of the privileged merchant class. Like any of us, many of his interests and the personal qualities exhibited in his early life reflect the age in which he lived.

As the child of a local successful merchant, Francis would have enjoyed the comforts and privileges preserved for those of wealth. Capable of both speaking and singing in French, probably through the efforts of his mother whose family came from France, the young Francis grew up to be familiar with French poetry, songs and traditions, as well as those of his native Umbria. From this background he was to absorb the then fashionable language of romantic courtly love and we can begin to understand how so adeptly, he later took the words of the gospels and turned them into chivalric poetry.

The town of Assisi, then as now, had its own bishop and cathedral church. The Church would have been an ever-present force

throughout Francis' early life. For instance, one can still see the font in the cathedral Church of San Rufino where around 1182, Francis was baptised. No doubt, there would have been the family prayers led by his devout mother, Pica and as a young boy, Francis would have most likely been educated by the clergy within his local parish. Whatever was learned and experienced within the Christian faith in those early years appears to have had little impact upon the daily preoccupations of the young Francis; that was yet to come.

From the earliest biography of Thomas of Celano we learn something of how Francis spent his youth. Thomas comments that, 'Until he was nearly twenty-five he squandered his time terribly. Indeed, he outshone all his friends in trivialities, suggested various evils, and was eager for foolishness of every kind'. The anxiety he may have caused his family during these adolescent years, however, was of little significance compared to that which was yet to occur.

PIETRO BERNADONE, FRANCIS' FATHER, was a very successful Assisi cloth merchant, who had also become a substantial property holder. Pica, his mother, almost certainly was from Provence, in the extreme southeast of Mediterranean France.

Pietro was wealthy and powerful. In stories about the life of Francis, he is uniformly portrayed in a negative fashion. Uncomprehending, unsupportive and untouched by any of the spirit of what was happening to his son, he is a somewhat grim figure. Nonetheless, it is hard not to feel just a little sympathy for him. Having a saint for a son could not have been easy. His wife did better. Indeed, in some of the stories she emerges as a character similar to Elizabeth, mother of John the Baptist, or perhaps the long suffering Monica, mother of Augustine. Pica was a romantic and loved music. She was said to have been devout and good.

Pietro specialised in the sale of French and Flemish fabrics of the best quality. His purchasing travels took him frequently to France. Assisi was itself on the main travel route between Rome and the North. Francis would certainly have joined his father on some of these journeys, especially since he was being groomed to take over the business by his early twenties. Pietro was frequently away from home, including at the time when Francis was born and also when Pica finally gave Francis permission to leave home to pursue a life with the Church.

Biographers from the early years are quick to contrast the easy-going, spendthrift years of Francis' youth with what happened after his conversion at the age of twenty-four, and are quick to blame his parents.

Family connections were to save him though. The civil war that was to see Francis imprisoned in Perugia in 1202–3 was an immensely complex affair. On the losing side, Francis was spared having his throat cut, only because his costly equipment indicated that he was a man of means worthy of a ransom payment. And eventually his father was to see to that.

His family background gave him personal assurance and the experience of extensive travel. His later dogged and steady determination, and his exuberantly impulsive goodwill each show something of what he had inherited from his two parents. These qualities were to serve him well.

Assisi then and now

THERE HAS BEEN A SETTLEMENT IN ASSISI for some 1700 years. The very name of the church in the main square tells us that story – Santa Maria Sopra Minerva – formerly a temple to the Roman goddess Minerva. The first Christian bishop of the town was martyred here. San Rufino's, the cathedral church at the town centre, proudly honours him. At the top end of the town, the unmistakeable oval shape of the Roman circus is heavily built over with medieval houses.

The town that Francis knew is still largely here. There are the externally modest but still substantial town houses for the nobility on the small squares. Lower down there are many narrow winding streets with small shops that have housing on the floors above. Supportive archways and buttresses, steps and staircases are everywhere a feature of this town (of some 5000 or so inhabitants) which was built on a steep hillside.

At times of festival there are continuing reminders that the town once divided into several competitive quarters. The costumes, the banners, the drums and the flags tossed high in the air with all their flashing colours, are quite magnificent. The two ruined parts of the defensive castle remain on the top of the ridge. In Francis' time this was fought over, several times. The town walls are tall and strong, and the gates are narrow. The huge complex that is the Basilica of San Francesco now dominates the western

end at the bottom of the steep ridge. Everywhere there are the towers and bells of churches and religious houses.

Assisi has always been a beautiful hill town in a charming part of the country. It remains so. Now on lazy summer days, visitors might find the town band playing on roughly cut grass by the castle wall, or in the piazza, just by the fountain. That would be so in a hundred such towns. But the continuing presence and appeal of Assisi's saint remains the one special addition that the others cannot match.

Assisi generally keeps cars and buses out of its narrow inner streets and lanes. But outside the walls it is quite different. There are hundreds of tour buses. Pilgrims coming by train can come from either of the two main north-south lines. Taxis do a roaring trade. So do the local buses. If travellers look young enough, their fare is determined by how tall they are! If the weather is good, some hardy types walk. They might regret that decision in the last steep parts of the climb. But they come to Assisi, not for the town band or even for the soft beauty of the rose-white stonework. They come, some four million a year, for Francis and for what Francis is seen to represent.

Clare

THE OTHER SAINT THAT IS INSEPARABLY associated with both Francis and Assisi is Chiara di Favarone. Known to us as Clare, she was some eleven or twelve years younger than Francis. Though their family homes were less than five minutes from each other, the lives of the noble Assisi families were very different. Francis lived the life of the merchant class while Clare lived a life of nobility.

They moved in different circles, though they attended mass at the same church at San Rufino. Clare lived in one of the grand houses facing onto the cathedral piazza. By the time she was six, the civil battles that were tearing Assisi apart had seen the house burnt and sacked and the extended family fleeing to Perugia. This was at the same time that Francis, an eager young cavalryman, was getting himself into serious trouble fighting on the other side.

Clare was born in 1193 or 1194, the eldest of three daughters to Favarone di Offreduccio, himself the younger brother of the leading nobleman of the town. Her mother, Ortolana, was also of the nobility. She had earlier travelled extensively on pilgrimages to Rome and to the Holy Land. Ortolana was well-educated and made sure that her daughters received the same benefit. Clare was therefore well-versed in Latin, history and literature. Because of the troubles brought on by the civil battles, the family was not to return to Assisi until around 1207.

The stories of Clare's life speak of the quiet and careful exis-

tence of an intelligent young woman, beautiful, devout and generous to the poor. In the normal scheme of things she would be being prepared for a useful and well-connected marriage at a reasonably early age. Several sources indicate though, that she was very interested in exploring the implications of a deeper spiritual life.

As it happened, just at this time Francis had returned from Rome as a deacon and was regularly preaching at the cathedral, San Rufino, almost next door to Clare's home. Sunday by Sunday she and her family heard and saw the group of friars, mostly locals, led by Francis and now living outside the town at the Portiuncula Chapel.

On several occasions, accompanied by one of her family servants who herself was to become a sister, Clare had secret meetings with Francis. It was becoming very clear that it was the religious life that was her vocation. But just when and indeed how was the question? After the death of her father, her uncle gained authority over her. Clare was considered a family asset and breaking away was not to be easy. Her family fought hard to keep her on the path of a conventional life. But Clare had inherited the strength and the ability to carry through her forming intentions. She wished as a woman, to live with other women, a life that was similar in devotion and sacrifice to that being lived by the man she admired and loved more than any other: Francis.

CHAPTER TWO

A Call to Community

IN ASSISI THE VISITORS AND CITIZENS, like the world at large, continue to bear testimony to the encounter of God with his people. Among the numerous passers-by following the Via San Francesco  from the basilica to the Piazza Communale are priests, religious and ordinary men and women who testify not only to a personal experience of God, but in some cases to a call or vocation. Some live within the walls of the town. Many others come from their various situations in life and numerous vocations as part of their search, their faith or perhaps in their own personal quest for a meaning to life.

Some come simply to enjoy the physical sites and surroundings significant to Francis and Clare, their fellow companions from an earlier age; others to learn more about their lives. Some have come to make a particular pilgrimage to the shrines of the two saints, or perhaps as a religious to spend some time within one of the many religious communities dotted throughout the town. Regardless of the reason, the primary focus of the town today

remains centred around these two great saints, Francis and Clare, who continue to bear witness to God who enters the lives of his people. Their own response to God's call and the radical new life that ensued, has seen them identified with the town of Assisi ever since.

It remains a mystery why one is called to the exclusion of another – Israel rather than any other nation, Mary as opposed to any other young Nazarene woman, the twelve disciples chosen by Jesus as opposed to any others – we can go on. An understanding of vocation has grown out of our experience of God as the one who calls. Without exception the prophets of ancient times, the apostles of the New Testament and the myriad of saints and martyrs who have followed have all believed themselves to be called by this one and same God.

In the town of Assisi around 1203, a young man's life too was gradually being transformed. A year in prison and convalescence, subsequent to his release, saw a turning point in his life. Francis

was slowly coming to the realisation that he was being called to a very different life. As his life slowly changed, the hallmarks of the Franciscan spirit began to be embodied in all that he said and did: simplicity of life, a desire to completely identify with Christ and a deep love and reverence for the created world, expressed through a spirit of joy and total self-giving.

Conversion

WHEN FRANCIS WAS IN HIS EARLY TWENTIES Assisi was at war with the neighbouring larger city of Perugia. Like all those of his age and social position, he was expected to be involved. He took part in the fighting and was imprisoned for a prolonged period. In an experience similar to that of the later St Ignatius Loyola, Francis was to find this cumulative experience the start of a conversion process. When he finally returned, his personality seemed changed – he was much more reflective and introverted.

This was the begining of his conversion. It was the starting point of a new life of radical Christian vision and reform. It was a new way and a challenging example that was to have a lasting impact both inside and beyond the Church. In another generation, this could have been the start of a Reformation and a divisive breach. In this, it brought astonishing renewal.

Francis turned aside from the comfortable life of the son of a prosperous merchant. That life would have essentially kept him in the centre of town, apart from the marginalised – the poor, the refugees, the homeless and the diseased. The turning around of his life was marked by some striking actions – three key steps that were central markers for his new direction. The first would have been deeply shocking to any who saw it. The second would have been incomprehensible to most. The third could well have left many shaking their heads.

The first was his reaching out to the most marginalised people of all – the lepers. Every community had them, banished from any normal social contact and waiting to die. Francis was suddenly struck by the conviction that his reaction of revulsion to such a person was a direct distortion of the gospel. The extravagant impulsiveness of his response was typical. He not only spoke and embraced the outcasts, he kissed both their hands and lips, and gave them money, and not once, but many times. As  he said himself:

> The Lord granted me, Brother Francis, to begin to do penance in this way. While I was in sin, it seemed very bitter to me to see lepers. And the Lord himself led me amongst them and I had mercy on them. And when I left them that which seemed bitter to me was changed into sweetness of soul and body.

A second extravagant gesture saw him selling up all of his father's fine cloth supplies. This resulted in a complete breach with his family. The famous fresco in the Upper Basilica at Assisi shows this – a naked Francis giving his very clothes back to his outraged father and being covered by the bishop's cloak. The proceeds of the sale of cloth were intended to go towards the third dramatic action. Francis started to rebuild.

At the ruined Church of San Damiano, down the hill outside Assisi, Francis found God and a vocation. He believed that in that ruined church, God called him to start rebuilding. And so he did. But the scope of the rebuilding was far beyond what he initially thought. The rebuilding was of the Church as a whole institution. This was a task he was to find others eager to join him in.

The
Early
Community

THE FORMATIVE EXPERIENCES AT WORK in Francis' conversion helped him come to see his future ministry as a shared task. At the Portiuncula Chapel on the Feast of St Matthias in 1208, Francis heard the account of Jesus' commission to his twelve disciples. They were to go out in pairs to fulfil the Lord's work. These words of Jesus resonated with Francis' own understanding of his calling so that they became, as it were, his manifesto. He responded to that commission himself, literally, and dared to preach and live that way in his home town.

The challenge to Francis, 'Preach as you go', began to bear fruit. Alone, without shoes, and clad in a ragged habit girded by a rope, he witnessed to his Lord. In doing so, despite the hardships and humiliation, he attracted other followers who sought to share his life. It was not long before he, too, was organising his followers to go out in pairs to fulfil the task that was given to the first disciples.

Among the first to be drawn to Francis' energy and vision was Bernardo di Quintavalle, a nobleman from Assisi. An invitation to come to Bernardo's house provided further opportunity for Francis to speak well into the night about his life and vision. The next morning Bernardo decided to give all his goods to the poor. Another local figure, Pietro di Catanio, a lawyer known to both Francis and Bernardo was also drawn to follow Francis' example.

These two also resolved to pattern their lives by the gospel, discarding their shoes and adopting the now distinctive habit. A community was being born.

The small group established itself at the Portiuncula Chapel at Santa Maria degli Angeli, on the plain below Assisi. This was to become their home. Here, another restoration project began. Santa Maria, unlike the huge basilica today, was an abandoned tumbledown chapel located in the woods. The Abbey of San Benedetto, owners of the chapel, were no doubt grateful for the labour that Francis and his companions offered. There, they built a simple hut and continued the restoration of the chapel, preaching and attending to the sick.

Within a few years following Francis' initial response to the gospel that was preached at the Portiuncula Chapel on that St Matthias Day, the community had grown to the biblical precedent of twelve. Among them were Thomas of Celano, Francis' first biographer and Silvester, the first priest within the community. Francis' personal inspiration, charisma and deep faith won through. Motivated by his trust in God and committed to his vision, there gradually emerged among the brethren a pattern of life. Without possessions, wandering through the villages and towns, preaching and ministering to the sick, they were totally dependent upon the generosity of others. Their first journey took them as far as the Marches on the central East Coast, after which they returned to Assisi continuing to live their simple, devout life.

Obviously with the growth of the community, a rule or code of behaviour became necessary. Francis wrote what was to become the First Rule for the brethren based on his early experiences and his understanding of their calling to the religious life. He also sought to gain approval from the Church.

FORMAL OFFICIAL CHURCH RECOGNITION as a religious order was not easily or quickly obtained. Such recognition was the Church's seal of approval. It affirmed the worthiness of the way of life proposed. It honoured the charism of the founder. It asserted the orthodoxy of the doctrine declared in The Rule and lived out by those who adopted it. It implied support and encouragement. But it also necessarily involved submission to the authority of the Church.

Francis knew all that, but he wanted to offer this new vision of what the Church might be to those at the very top of the structures. That meant, with the approval and the encouragement of his own bishop in Assisi, going directly to Rome.

In the volatile political and religious climate of the time, this was the best way to attempt to avoid the accusation of heresy. Otherwise this new movement could have been suppressed, perhaps with the same violence that had destroyed other such brotherhoods. At the same time Francis was definitely making it clear that the two main existing structures for religious orders at the time – Augustinian and Benedictine – were either too settled or too comfortable for what was needed.

What he wanted and saw to be necessary was a new order with a different rule, structure and purpose, utterly centred on the life and precepts of Jesus Christ himself. What a challenge that repre-

sented. What a challenge that continues to present, 800 years later. This directness of purpose is a quality that still attracts, inspires and humbles.

In 1209 Francis and his twelve companions went to Rome to seek Pope Innocent III's blessing and approval. Against the odds, they were heard, first by officials and a sympathetic cardinal, and then by the Pope himself. The process lasted several days. The  Pope had had a disturbing dream a couple of nights before. A crumbling Lateran basilica was only saved from falling by resting on one small man. He came to realise that this man was Francis. Again this scene is depicted in one of the great frescoes in the Upper Basilica in Assisi. Francis stated his case:

The King of Kings has told me that he will provide for all the sons he raises up through me, because if he cares for strangers he will also look after his own children. Since he gives so many of the good things of life to the unworthy and sinners, he will provide even more generously for those who spread his message. Please, therefore, confirm our rule taken from the gospels.

And the Pope gave his support: 'We approve your rule. Go, Brothers with the Lord, and preach penitence to everyone, in whatever way he inspires you.'

Francis promised 'obedience and reverence' to the Pope and the brothers in turn promised the same to Francis. It was agreed that Francis would be ordained a deacon. So began this new order of friars – fratres minores – the little brothers. The proceedings of the Lateran Council in 1215 were to confirm this.

Clare
in her
Community

1212 SAW THE FOUNDATION OF A SECOND ORDER of Franciscans, for women. Under his inspiration and guidance, Chiara di Favarone, at the age of eighteen, was to follow where the twenty-nine year old Francis was leading. Throughout the rest of his life they were the closest of friends and companions. Her example in turn was to inspire and to attract many women.

On the evening of Palm Sunday 1212, Clare left Assisi, with the assistance of the bishop. She went down the hill to the Portiuncula where the friars were waiting. She was welcomed there by the friars bearing flaming torches. Francis had already been to Rome to discuss this expansion of the scope of the Order. Clare was received, and took a vow of obedience to Francis. Her hair was shaved. Her mother's older companion went with her, as shortly too did her own blood sister, who took the religious name of Agnes.

Later, in 1253, at the time of the proceedings leading up to Clare's canonisation, there were still a dozen of the then young girls who had followed Clare into the religious life, well able to testify to her heroic nature in those early days. All of them were part of the group that had been so inspired by Francis' preaching at the cathedral. Women in need or seeking a vocation were always welcome at their sanctuary. San Damiano was to remain their home for the next forty years.

One of the stories that emerged in the 1253 hearings spoke of Clare's great courage and leadership at a time of warfare when there was no one at all to defend the convent. The story is still told today to every pilgrim who comes to San Damiano. The round window above the modest main entrance to the convent and church is where in 1240 Clare held high the monstrance containing the consecrated bread of the Body of the Lord. That was the only protection she and her sisters had in the face of an attacking band of Arab mercenaries – that and her formidable personality and iron determination. The mercenaries left. No one who was there ever forgot that moment.

From the beginning the Poor Clares were blessed with vocations. Within a few years there were fifty sisters at San Damiano and there was a second house in Spello nearby.

Following the 1215 Fourth Lateran Council, Innocent III affirmed their special call:

> Innocent…to the beloved daughters in Christ, Clare and other handmaidens of the Church of San Damiano of Assisi, both present and future, professing in perpetuity life according to a rule…As you have asked we, with apostolic favour, approve your aim of highest poverty, granting with the authority of this writing, that by no one may you be forced to receive possessions.

Innocent IV was to formalise this in The Rule of 1253, finally given to Clare on her death-bed. For most of her life she had to fight to retain the original vision for this second order.

CHAPTER THREE

The Spirit of Francis

NO DOUBT MANY OF US, INCLUDING THOSE WHO have made the journey to Assisi, have pondered the question of the extraordinary appeal of Francis. Even 800 years later, we recognise that he brought something radically new to the life of the Church. His reverence for the natural world and the spirit of joy and confidence with which he embraced the Christian Gospel have continued to speak to every generation. The fact that he continues to attract and inspire those within and beyond the family of faith, testifies to the timeless nature of his message and his commitment to the fundamentals of life.

A legacy of many of the great saints has been their ability to reveal yet another dimension of our understanding of the Christian faith and how we express it in our lives. St Benedict, St Seraphim of Sarov, St Thérèse of Lisieux and St John of the Cross, to name just a few, have each in their individual way contributed to our own understanding of God, through his Church. Each one of them also, has influenced how others have subsequently understood their

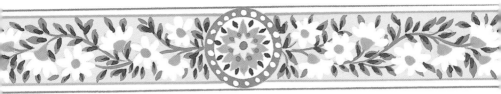

own personal experience in the light of faith, have expressed their inner spiritual life and lived out their own response to the Christian Gospel.

So too, with Francis, and his spirit lives on. His message and particular understanding of the life of faith continues to speak to us in numerous ways. There is the radical and uncompromising response he makes to the Gospel. From the very outset in response to the challenge Christ offers his disciples in Matthew 10:7-13, Francis accepts the words literally and lives  his life in total dependence upon the promises of Christ. His continual quest in life 'to put on Christ' and embrace Sister Poverty continue to fill us with awe and admiration. We are not all called to such a radical response to the teachings of Christ. Nevertheless, Francis' utter trust in God and his simplicity of life have continued to attract others and subsequently bring many to a deeper understanding of their life in faith.

There is also the irresistible appeal of Francis through his profound love of the natural world, so touchingly recorded in his own words and those of his followers. His own 'The Canticle of Brother Sun' or the host of stories collected in *The Little Flowers* written soon after his death testify to an individual who saw the goodness of God in all aspects of human life as well as through all creation. This total self-giving, the relentless quest to place Christ at the centre of all, whatever the cost, to see the providence of God in all things, remain for Francis an occasion for joy and thanksgiving.

The
Crucifix
Prayer

IN 1206 SAN DAMIANO WAS FALLING INTO RUIN. This was one of a number of such places that the young Francis was visiting more and more. Inside the church was a large Byzantine style cross – almost life size, brightly coloured and two-dimensional; an icon rather than a statue. The Lord on this cross was not yet dead. The face was alert and searching, with 'resigned serenity' as one writer has put it.

It was before this crucifix that Francis was praying one spring morning. As is recorded in the tradition, Francis went away from that church filled with great joy. Jesus had spoken directly to him. The Lord of the cross had spoken to him with tenderness, calling him to rebuild a church that was falling down.

He was filled with this image of Christ and his suffering and felt powerfully that he was being called to identify himself with that suffering. The man who wrote the crucifix prayer of complete trust in God was the one most earnestly searching for direction in his vocation, while bursting with an awareness of God's love turning his life around.

ALL-highest, glorious God,
cast your light
into the darkness of my heart.

Give me right faith,
firm hope, perfect charity,
and profound humility,
wisdom and perception,
so that I may do what is
truly your holy will.
Amen.

The Rule

THE REVISED RULE OF 1221 (THE SECOND RULE) ultimately captures the spirit of Francis. Sadly, the earlier text of the First Rule has been lost and the much modified later Rule of 1223 became the rule that was adopted by the Order.

The Rule of 1221, however, provides a more personal insight into Francis. Written in a more intimate style, it tells us as much about the founder of a new religious order as about the man totally dependent upon the promises of Christ. It is perhaps this conviction above all, that permeates this particular version of the Rule.

The author never moves far from the source of his own personal call and inspiration. His exhortations to his brothers, as well as his personal vision of the Franciscan life, are often illustrated by numerous quotes from the gospels and sayings of Jesus.

The final rule approved by Pope Honorius III in 1223 was essentially a compromise. Modified because of divergent views about the future of the Order, it is a much briefer document shaped to provide practical and clear guidance for the Order. Unchanged since that time, it continues to shape the life of the Order to the present day. Here are some key excerpts.

The whole idea of the life of the brothers
is to follow the example of Christ
by a life of obedience, chastity, and freedom
from all material possession.

Brothers…should seek the most humble jobs so that they are on the lowest rung of the economic ladder. They should be servants rather than masters.

If the brethren are gathered for a meeting,
they should be hospitable and cheerful.
There should be no hypocritical appearance of poetry
or asceticism. In short, they should be
happy, joyful, and gracious as befitting
followers of the Lord.

The brothers who are anxious to follow
the humility and poverty of our Lord Jesus Christ
should allow themselves only what the Apostle
permits: 'Having food and something to cover
ourselves with, we consider ourselves content.'
The brothers should consider it a privilege to live with
the outcasts of this world: the sick, the weak, the poor
lepers, and the beggars on the road.

The
Christmas
Crib

WE ARE ALL FAMILIAR WITH THE NATIVITY SETS that appear around Christmas time on mantle pieces, in parish churches and in public spaces. What might be less well-known is that this practice and public devotion comes to us from Francis. In a little community called Greccio, on a river valley not so far from Assisi, Francis had one of his favourite places of retreat. There were many small communities of brothers in the valley and most of the local farming people were following the Franciscan way. This included gathering together with great joy to celebrate the festival of Christmas. So far as Francis was concerned, this was a celebration that should include all God's creatures. For instance, he was not happy with the tradition of trapping and eating larks as a great specialty for that day. Rather, he thought extra grain should be spread so they too could join the feast. And the other animals deserved attention too:

> Out of reverence for the Son of God…all men ought to give a good meal to our brothers the oxen and asses on Christmas Eve. Similarly on Christmas Day the poor ought to be handsomely fed by the rich.

It was towards the end of his life that Francis gave us all this wonderful inclusive devotion, which is the honouring of the birth of the Lord accompanied by those creatures present. But our own nativity scenes are but a pale shadow of that first occasion. In 1223 at

Greccio, the whole valley gathered for an outdoor mass celebrated at that specially constructed, fully stocked stable, built at Francis' direction next to the hermitage. Ox, ass, sheep and hay were all there. Francis was the deacon for the mass, preaching about each of the animals present, as well as about the Christ Child, his mother and all the others. There was joy, light and celebration. This saw the start of a practice that remains to this day.

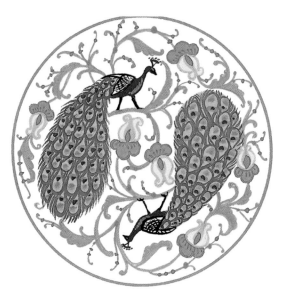

The
Little
Flowers

THE LITTLE FLOWERS, I FIORETTI, is a substantial collection of stories, teachings and chronicles. They are now readily available in the public domain for anybody who searches. They remain one of the best early sources of much that is told to us about Francis and Clare and the early community. They breathe the spirituality of those who love God in the Franciscan tradition. They speak clearly of the infectious attraction that the deliberate return to the very basics of the faith had.

Readers are informed of how the word spread, and even if perhaps there is more than a little gilding of the lily, readers can still see and share in the love that the collectors and writers of these many 'little flowers' so clearly had, both for the chief characters and for God.

The 'flowers' together form a great floral decoration to celebrate the power and grace of God most wonderfully at work. The stories are charming and without any pretence to intellectual complexity or sophistication, yet they engage readers and encourage them to go deeper in their own search for God. God is honoured and the disciple is encouraged. After nearly 800 years, *The Little Flowers* are still beautifully fresh.

THE PREACHING TO THE BIRDS

THE STORY OF THE PREACHING TO THE BIRDS is one particularly loved tale, recorded in a giant fresco in the main basilica in Assisi. Chapter XVI of *The Little Flowers* contains this description of Francis' search to understand just what God wanted of him. Should he devote himself entirely to prayer? Should he preach and travel widely? The answer came that he was not called for his own sake only, but also for the salvation of others, and that included the birds. As the standard translation has it:

> And entering into the field, he began to preach to the birds which were on the ground, and suddenly all those also on the trees came round him, and all listened while St Francis preached to them, and did not fly away until he had given them his blessing.

His sermon called on them to give praise and thanks to God, as all creatures should because of what God had provided. The narrative continues:

> As he said these words, all the birds began to open their beaks, to stretch their necks, to spread their wings and reverently to bow their heads to the ground, endeavouring by their motions and by their songs to manifest their joy to St Francis. And the

saint rejoiced with them. He wondered to see such a multitude of birds, and was charmed with their beautiful variety, with their attention and familiarity, for all which he devoutly gave thanks to the Creator.

After receiving Francis' blessing of the Sign of the Cross, readers are told that the birds themselves flew off in four directions, themselves making the Sign of the Cross in the sky. This was a celebration and a statement about the nature of a central Franciscan theme: Be joyfully aware of God's love and care for you. Respond with thanks, and spread that love and care as widely as you are able. Show the difference this good news makes, with a merry heart.

The explosion in the number of those in all three orders of this new movement, even in that first generation when these stories were being collected, would see this message and this particular spirituality spreading far and wide. More often than not, just like with the birds, the enterprise was seen to be relying only on the providence of God.

THE WOLF OF GUBBIO

THERE ARE MANY WONDERFUL STORIES ABOUT the life of Francis. Like all good stories, some of them have grown in the telling. Francis did so much in a relatively short time. He made such a difference to the lives of so many people that those who had had first-hand contact cherished the small details of what he said and did. His way was different. While Francis was still alive, many were saying that at last there was someone who lived and loved like Jesus did. So as with Jesus, stories grew around particular incidents. And they were always stories which left a message about how to behave, how to reach out to others, or how to love God and all of God's creations.

The story of the fearsome wolf of Gubbio is one of these stories. In the narrative Francis brings peace and contentment to the heart of a wild and tormented animal – and helps a whole community.

As the story goes, Francis was called to Gubbio. The town is not far from Assisi by car, but it took a couple of days to walk over the steep hills. A fierce wolf had taken up residence in a cave near the town and had all the citizens terrified. Wolves could and frequently did eat people 800 years ago in Europe. A sturdy baker's wife dusted with flour was said to have been the only one of the

townspeople brave enough to take Francis up to the cave. Here the story reminds readers of the early Roman story about Androcles and the Lion where the love and care of a Christian saint for another of God's creatures makes the difference. We are told that Francis and the wolf had an earnest conversation. The result was that Brother Wolf and Brother Francis came down the hill together. Instead of being a threat, the wolf became the protector of the town and lived to a great age.

The way of Francis was an alternative way that earned respect from popes, birds, wolves, sultans and all sorts of ordinary people. The stories about him continue to live to this day.

The
Canticle of
Brother Sun

DURING A TIME OF CONVALESCENCE at San Damiano in 1225, Francis composed one of his most famous and best loved works. He gave this collection of praises the title The Canticle of Brother Sun. Reminiscent in its refrain of praise to the Christian hymn, 'The Benedicite', it is a highly original work and is distinctively Franciscan.

Simple, yet so profound. Poetic in style, yet so accessible. It represents one of the earliest poems written in the Italian language and became an instant success. Through the opening words, a salutation to God, Francis leads us through a series of praises for God's works in creation which, in an entirely novel way, recognises humankind's relationship with creation as that of a family. 'Brother Sun' and 'Sister Moon', water, wind, air and earth are not to be subdued as in Genesis, but rather to be loved and cherished as our own kin.

It is little surprise that this work is seen as prophetic, even today. Francis shares with us a vision of a world that is totally interdependent, where creation, in all its beauty and power, demands our respect. The miracles of night and day, the seasons in their various forms and the rich bounty of Mother Earth are cause for continual praise and thanksgiving.

ost high, omnipotent, good Lord
to you alone belong praise and glory,
honor, and blessing.
No man is worthy to breathe your name.

Be praised, my Lord,
for all your creatures.

In the first place for
the blessed Brother Sun
who gives us the day
and enlightens us through you.

He is beautiful and radiant
with his great splendor,
giving witness of you,
most omnipotent One.

e praised, my Lord, for Sister Moon
and the stars
formed by you so bright,
precious, and beautiful.

Be praised, my Lord, for Brother Wind
and the airy skies, so cloudy and serene;
for every weather, be praised,
for it is life-giving.

Be praised, my Lord, for Sister Water
so necessary yet so humble,
precious, and chaste.

Be praised, my Lord, for Brother Fire,
who lights up the night.
He is beautiful and carefree, robust
and fierce.

Be praised, my Lord, for our sister,
Mother Earth,
who nourishes and watches us
while bringing forth abundant fruits
with colored flowers and herbs.

Be praised, my Lord, for those who pardon
through your love
and bear weakness and trial.
Blessed are those who endure in peace
for they will be crowned by you, Most High.

Amen.

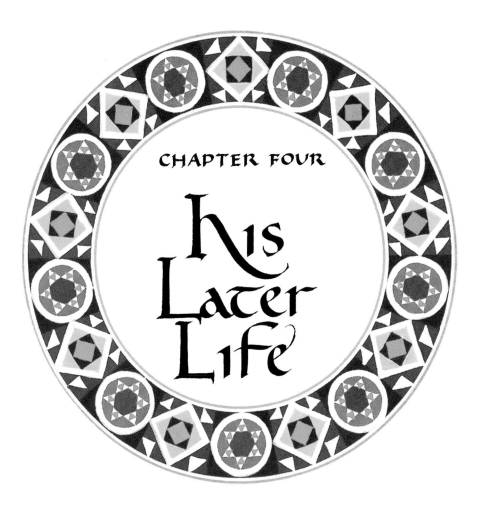

CHAPTER FOUR

His
Later
Life

OSCAR WILDE WROTE OF FRANCIS in his work *De Profundis*, 'God had given him at his birth the soul of a poet, and he himself when quite young had in mystical marriage taken Poverty as his bride'.

 Francis' latter years were marked by the inevitable tension between the poet, the visionary and the ascetic with that of the responsibility for the overseeing of a rapidly growing community. He was no administrator. By the time he had decided to leave the administration to others in 1220, his number of followers within the community had grown to several thousand spread over much of Europe and with missionaries also dispatched to the Holy Land and North Africa. While he was prepared to hand the responsibility of overseeing to others, he was always anxious to see the community remain faithful to the original precepts as established in those first years – to live simply and to identify with the poor.

Despite the problems relating to the ongoing organisation of the brotherhood, his latter years proved to be a period of enormous energy and inspiration. As throughout his earlier years, he found consolation in retreating to places of isolation where he could spend time in prayer and meditation. 'The Last Testament', written towards the end of his life, is a deeply personal message written to his brethren reminding them of the fundamentals that bind them together, and a plea that they remain faithful to their teaching. Francis writes:

> All my brothers, clerical and lay, are ordered in obedience to make glosses neither on the rule nor on these words…rather, as the Lord told me what to say and how to write this rule purely and simply, they are to observe this rule and these words simple and purely and fulfil them right to the end.

He continued to inspire by example. There was the constant need to preach which often meant completing entire journeys not only within his native Umbria but the Marches and southern Italy, as well as the occasion in 1218 before Pope Honorius III and the cardinals of the Holy College. There was also his eventful visit to

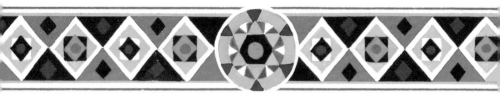

the East. We need to remember that such journeys and continuing witness to his Lord were accomplished while living in abject poverty, begging for food and experiencing the austerities that this personal view of the gospel imposed. There was also the constant need to care for the sick and poor wherever he went.

Having taken 'Poverty for his Lady', he was slowly worn out by the austerities he himself imposed. The vision and stigmata experienced during a retreat on Mount La Verna only added to his failing health. However, even times of recuperation such as with the Poor Clares, a year prior to his death, provided the occasion for him to offer a hymn of praise to God as recorded in 'The Canticle of Brother Sun'. 'Sister Death' was not far away.

His
Visit to
the East

THE EARLY EASTERN CHURCH and the example of the Desert Fathers were already known to Francis. The Tau Cross, used by St Anthony of Egypt and of such ancient origin, was Francis' own preferred symbol. He used it by his signature in letters, as a sort of seal. His walking staff, on which he increasingly had to rely, was the same 'Greek Cross'. It is to be found in some of the caves he used as hermitages. The East then, was for him where the Western Church met its own simple origins, as well as the Saracens.

The battles he had to fight even within his own order were battles about how to find, to know and to serve God. The practical, the pragmatic and the reasonable were confused by this, but this in part explains Francis' distrust of learning and of scholarly pursuits. They could become ends in themselves, goals that only distance their pursuers from the God they would honour. Was Francis to discuss such burning problems with the mystics and visionaries of Islam and the monks of the Eastern Church?

Like most other devout believers of his time with the resources to do it, Francis was keen to go to the Holy Land. He took a dozen brothers with him, to extend the work there. He was to attract many new brothers. But this was in a particularly grim part of the Fifth Crusade. By 1219 only a few isolated outposts remained in Christian hands. Francis and his brothers found themselves immersed in the pastoral care of the troops – nursing and preach-

ing. They went with the crusader forces besieging a key Arab port city on the Nile delta. Damietta had a population of some 80,000. In the end almost all were to die and the survivors were to be sold into slavery. Meanwhile, disease, floods, and slaughter in battle were taking a terrible toll on both sides. The Christian forces had just suffered a humiliating defeat, and the city remained untaken. The stalemate continued, at appalling human cost.

It is a matter of record that Francis and one other brother walked through the drawn-up battle lines. Francis wished to speak to the sultan. His intention was to convert him if he could and in any case to stop the fighting with an agreed truce. The mission was so improbable and the pair of brothers so simple and tattered in their appearance that they were not killed on the spot, but taken through to the sultan's headquarters, not far from the city. Francis and the sultan were each to see in the other, one who was 'just, civilised and a man of peace.' As a result, Malik al-Kamil, the Sultan of Egypt, received Francis with respect and dignity over a period of several days. A decade later, access to Jerusalem for the crusaders was to be successfully negotiated with this same leader.

At the time, Francis had failed to convert the sultan and to bring about an end to the fighting. But he had offered another way. This has never been forgotten.

The
Stigmata

FOLLOWING HIS RETURN FROM THE EAST, the ongoing strain due to the administration of his brotherhood and the further pressure for reform of the community (that eventually led to the approval of the Confirmed Rule of 1223 by the papacy), took their toll. True to form, Francis sought refreshment in places of quiet and solitude, first in a cave near Greccio, and later in the decision to go into retreat at Mount La Verna.

Even for the modern pilgrim today travelling by car, Mount La Verna is remote, located high up in the Tuscan mountains. The shrine today perched high on a rocky cliff surrounded by a magnificent stand of trees and overlooking the valleys below, still radiates a profound sense of peace and awe, despite the constant stream of buses and crowds of pilgrims. It was there on September 14, 1224 (the Feast of the Holy Cross) that Francis experienced a mystical vision of Christ on the cross. It was no ordinary vision. Francis was transfixed by the vision of a six-winged seraph coming down from heaven with a crucified figure appearing in the middle of its wings. The moment is most poignantly caught in Giotto's fresco depicting the scene in the Church of Santa Croce in Florence. As recorded in Bonaventure's *Major Life*:

Francis, struck dumb by the vision, reacted with joy and sorrow: joy at the gracious look Christ gave him among the wings of the seraph and sorrow like a sword thrust that pierced his soul at

the sight of the figure affixed to a cross…As the vision receded from sight it left the saint's heart ablaze and imprinted upon his own body a miraculous likeness. Right then the marks of the nails began to appear in his body.

The stigmata, as it has come to be popularly known, is yet another of the extraordinary events surrounding the life of Francis. Not only was he the first to take the words of Christ literally, but also to endure in a most profound way the sufferings of Christ in his own person. Following the Mount La Verna vision, Francis' hands, feet and side bore the wounds similar to that of the crucified Christ. It was the first ever such recorded experience in the Christian West. Others have since followed, perhaps most notably in the last century, Padre Pio, himself a follower of the way of Francis.

This profound mystical experience and the suffering that ensued only exacerbated Francis' already failing health. While continuing to preach throughout Umbria and as far as the Marches his life and work were increasingly marked by the need for rest.

IN THE WINTER OF 1225 FRANCIS STAYED with the Poor Clares at San Damiano's for eight weeks. He was completely blind and nearly helpless, but still able to compose and to sing 'The Canticle of Brother Sun', and to teach it to his brothers.

For some weeks in 1226 he stayed at the bishop's palace in Assisi. There he found peace and comfort in his realisation that 'Sister Death' was near. Though some thought it unseemly, he was full of joy at this. He gathered his brothers to sing to him and he added a new and what would be the last verse to the canticle.

Be praised, my Lord, for our Sister Bodily Death,
from whom none can escape that has drawn breath…
Praise and bless my Lord, and do him service due,
With humblest thanks for all he has done for you.

In late September 1226, Francis asked that he be carried back down to the Portiuncula. Half way down that familiar hill, held and supported by his brothers, he gave a final blessing to the Assisi he loved, even though he could no longer see it. Clare herself was too ill at that time to come to him. But to ease her distress, Francis sent a loving message to her and her sisters. Another long-time friend and benefactor, the Roman widow Giacoma de Settesoli, was allowed into the enclosure at Francis' express wish. She was to provide his burial clothes and some sweet marzipan cakes to delight him even then.

Shortly before he died, he had the brothers gather. He spoke of poverty and patience, and following the teachings of Christ. He broke bread, and blessed it and shared it with everyone present. Each person present received the hand of blessing, starting with the brothers who had first joined him.

On the evening of his death, October 3, 1226, at his insistence he was placed naked on the bare earth. John 13 was read:

> Now before the festival of the Passover, Jesus knew that his hour had come to depart from this world and go to the Father. Having loved his own who were in this world, he loved them to the end.

Francis was forty-four at the time of his death.

An ever-swelling crowd of the faithful and the curious were to spend the whole night praying, singing and waiting. In the morning, the huge crowd escorted the body slowly back up the hill. There were more prayers, more songs and finally trumpets. Branches were spread from the olive trees all along the way. At San Damiano, the coffin rested and was opened for Clare and her sisters to offer their farewell. Amidst great celebration, the requiem mass was offered at San Giorgio's, later to be the site of the basilica for Santa Chiara. Clare's requiem was held in the same church in 1253. Francis was canonised in 1228 as a saint of God.

CHAPTER FIVE

His
Legacy

TODAY, COUNTLESS VISITORS CONTINUE TO TRAVEL the winding road that leads up the hill through the medieval gates into the town of Assisi. Among them are the simply curious, the art student that 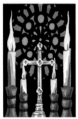 is there to examine the Giotto frescoes, and the omnipresent tourist who has come to see yet another Umbrian hill town.

However, the hundreds of lighted candles flickering before the saint's shrine in the crypt of the basilica testify to yet another kind of visitor – the continuous daily file of pious pilgrims seeking to visit the two great saints laid at rest within their shrines. They have come perhaps simply to look, but also to pray, to reflect and possibly to seek renewal and meaning in their own lives.

Francis continues to speak. His capacity for love, his utter commitment to the example of Christ, and his respect for all God's creatures have an enduring fascination. The simplicity of his message is compelling. His literal living out of the gospel imperatives of love, peace, compassion and forgiveness, in a spirit of joy, continue

to challenge and inspire. His prophetic message has a universal appeal. It is as relevant in today's world of international tensions, poverty and threat of environmental disaster as it was in the equally perilous medieval world of the thirteenth century.

The Franciscan message also continues to be embodied in the lives of those men and women who embrace the religious life in communities that continue to follow The Rule of St Francis or the contemplative life of the Poor Clares. It is significant that such religious communities are not only the preserve of the  Roman Catholic Church but also part of the Anglican tradition and part inspiration for various Protestant communities. Again, the saint and his message know no boundaries or religious divides. His message, which represents the very heart of the gospel, speaks to all peoples regardless of denomination, religion or race.

Francis saw God mirrored through all creation which engendered a deep reverence for all life and a child-like wonder for creation. Only such an appreciation and respect for the environment

will save today's world from the mounting ecological crises that face us. His love for both God and humanity were all-consuming. It led him not only to embrace the leper, clothe the poor and feed the hungry, but also to enter into dialogue with the enemy during the Crusades. The instability of our current international situation engenders both fear and suspicion. Francis' courageous gesture is a salutary reminder that in the words of St Paul, there is 'a still more excellent way'.

ENJOYING A MORNING COFFEE in the Piazza Communale, it is not surprising to note among the passers-by, the numerous religious marked by their distinctive dress. The town of Assisi includes numerous religious houses for both male and female communities. What is perhaps of some surprise, however, is that despite the variety of colours distinguishing the religious communities, almost all would belong to the Franciscan rule.

Visiting the shrine at the basilica, one notes the distinctive black habit of the friars who are housed in the impressive Sacro Convento immediately adjacent. They are also the custodians of the Carceri (Hermitage), located on the slopes of Mount Subasio high above the town of Assisi. It was a favourite place of retreat for Francis and remains a popular destination for pilgrims today.

On the other hand, attending the popular evening vespers at San Damiano located on the outskirts of the town, you are greeted by the young novices wearing the distinctive brown habit. This is perhaps the habit most closely identified with the Franciscans. In fact, the cappuccino enjoyed in the piazza is named after the distinctive brown robe of the Capuchin Friar.

Then there are also the grey habits of other Franciscan communities, more identified with the English Church, hence their English name Grey Friars.

The various habits testify to the different expressions of The

Rule and spirituality found in Franciscan religious life. All Franciscan religious, whether priest or brother, 'brown', 'black' or 'grey', commit themselves to God and the Church through the vows of poverty, chastity and obedience. They have branched out to every part of the world serving in numerous capacities to serve God as missionaries, chaplains, counsellors, social workers, health care workers, teachers and a host of other vocations.

The Franciscan found at the basilica in his distinctive black robe, belongs to the Conventual Franciscans. The term 'conventual' refers to their tendency to live in larger friaries. For instance, the friary refectory room at the basilica can accommodate 700 people, testifying to the significant presence of the Conventuals within the Franciscan movement over the centuries. The Conventuals continue to embrace two values of Franciscan life; namely, community and prayer. In their life and ministry they testify to the presence of God through Jesus in the same spirit as that which motivated Francis throughout his life.

Perhaps the most famous Franciscan belonging to the Conventuals would be the Polish martyr, Father Maximilian Kolbe. Canonised in 1981, his courage and deep compassion shown in the Nazi extermination camps, exemplify the spirit of Francis' love of God and desire to bring Christ to others.

The Capuchins, on the other hand, tend to live in small communities reminiscent of the early Franciscans, committed to small hermitages and functioning as wandering preachers. Today there are around 12,000 Capuchins living and working in fraternities in every part of the world, particularly in many undeveloped countries.

The
Poor Clares

THE BASILICA OF SANTA CHIARA IS ONE OF THE GREAT landmarks in Assisi. The earthquake of 1987 severely damaged the great enclosed convent. In the crypt church are the earthly remains of the saint who was Francis' great companion of the faith. One of Clare's sisters sits close by, completely and heavily veiled. The other great treasure here is the life sized Byzantine style crucifix that spoke to Francis. The crucifix has been moved here from San Damiano to provide pilgrims with easier access to it. In the chapel of the crucifix, to the side of the main church, another sister will sit, also completely veiled, black fabric over dark brown, handing out prayer cards to the pilgrims. These are the only Poor Clares you will see there, and they invite you to pray.

In another side chapel beside that of the great crucifix, the early morning mass is said. There is a wooden wall extending across the whole width. Out of sight, behind that wall is the sisters' chapel. From the other side, their voices respond to the prayers and chant the psalms. At the appropriate time, the priest brings the Blessed Sacrament through a small door from the sister's chapel. Our communion is their communion. Their early morning peace and grace is also ours.

By the time of Clare's death in 1253 there were already more than 150 communities spreading all over Europe. For those who look to Clare as their Mother Foundress, each monastic house

enjoys a considerable degree of autonomy. But they have much in common. As one of the communities puts it: 'In each house you will find that same spirit of simplicity and joy that is characteristic of all Franciscans.' And another declares, 'The charism of the Poor Clares is to be poor. Our life is an expression of the never failing providence of our Heavenly Father.'

This second order for women lives in an enclosure within the walls of a monastery, not leaving except for a 'manifest and reasonable cause', as is dictated by The Rule of St Clare. A regular day starts at 5.30 am. The round of prayers and mass, meals, work and recreation forms a steady and sustaining pattern. The chapel and the mass are at the centre of it all. The Poor Clares pray. They work with their hands, often making altar breads  and growing their own food. The simplicity of the life has a constant appeal. They live and work largely in silence.

They continue to attract vocations. In 2002 there were over 20,000 Poor Clares living in over seventy-six countries throughout the world.

By any reckoning, their life is hard and their Rule is strict. Yet this remains a part of the traditional Christian religious life that continues to flourish. Perhaps it is the example of Clare's remarkable strength of personality and conviction over so many years that is a key to understanding why this might be so. She too, as well as Francis, has had continuing influence throught the generations.

There are other active or non-contemplative orders for women that are Franciscan in ethos. Very close to the Basilica of Santa Chiara, for instance, the American Graymore sisters, clad in Franciscan brown, offer St Anthony's Guesthouse for pilgrims from throughout the world.

A Saint
for this
Age

WHEN IS A MEDIEVAL SAINT WHO CELEBRATES and honours the wild beauty of the natural order and who rejoices in the dignity of all creatures under God going to find a resurgence of interest? Now is one such time. Obviously this generation finds that Francis speaks to them. So did the poets and writers of the early nineteenth century romantic revival. Devout Christians had of course never forgotten Il Poverello from Umbria. The religious tradition he founded and the spirituality that he expressed and inspired had remained one of the most influential of all the traditions within Christianity. But it was his reputation outside the Church that was to change.

For nineteenth century and later spiritual and intellectual explorers, Francis' joyful celebration of the natural created order was exactly what they themselves were trying to do in poetry and art. These well-educated and literate Europeans of the North could aspire to join their Mediterranean cousins in a growing devotion and respect for the thirteenth century Italian hill town saint. A new awareness of this surprising and powerful figure within the Christian tradition also spread to North America and beyond. Francis was someone with something to say. He had an approach to life and to the world that was inspiring and yet somehow on the edge of the institutional Church. He was also appealing to those who were simply of goodwill.

The most popular representations of Francis are with animals or birds. He is placed in gardens or in secluded places of great beauty. He is seen to rejoice in all the created order. There is a joyful, evident care in all that he did.

It is easy to move from there to the broader concerns of the contemporary environmental movement. This very powerful intellectual movement could find an ally in Francis, if they felt so inclined.

The theology of it all is simple. Everything is equally under the care, concern and providence of God. The Christian will show love and respect. In our humanity, we ourselves are part of the wider greater ecology. If the birds are worthy of a sermon, then how much more are our fellow human beings worthier of even greater attention? Then there is the wind, the rain, the snow, the plants, the animals, the cold hard earth, our fellow human beings: rich or poor, sick or well, of the faith or not. We are all in this together.

In 1986 there was a major meeting of the leaders of the major world faiths and leaders of the environmental movement. The Worldwide Fund for Nature and religious leaders saw the point of calling such a meeting in Assisi. And they considered that the message of the Christian saint was a message that had broader appeal across the traditions of faith, and around the world. The impact of the truly radical nature of Francis' insight into the relationship of all created things with God, is powerful. Mother Teresa of Calcutta was said to see the Lord in the dying poor. She had the ability, as Francis did, to see God not only in all people, but in all.

THE NAME AND MESSAGE OF FRANCIS is invoked every time the 'Prayer of St Francis'(page 121) is said or sung, in whatever version or language.

The whole prayer is about contrasts. But just as in the Gospel of John, darkness cannot overwhelm the light, so here pardon and faith, hope and comfort, joyful giving and forgiveness, will result in life where otherwise there is death. In this prayer there is a complete pattern of living, offered up in thanksgiving.

Twice Pope John Paul II called the leaders of world religions to Assisi to speak together, to share hospitality. The first had been for the care of the environment, in 1986. The second time in January 2002 was to offer prayers for the peace of the world and for peace between the followers of different religious faiths, as well as the traditions within Christianity itself. In the latter gathering, John Paul II urged all believers to be 'lights of peace'. There was a sense of growing urgency and need, which was clearly acknowledged, and the immediate reason was quite apparent.

Significantly, this was just months after the events of September 11, 2001. The world had become more uncertain and there was a growing fear that a new phase of war and violence on a world scale was about to begin. A peace lamp was lit and passed around. A joint prayer was offered at the saint's tomb:

Violence never again! War never again! Terrorism never again!

ord, make me an instrument of your peace;
where there is hatred let me sow love,
where there is injury let me sow pardon,
where there is doubt let me sow faith,
where there is despair let me give hope,
where there is darkness let me give light,
where there is sadness let me give joy.

O Divine Master, grant that I may
not try to be comforted but to comfort,
not try to be loved but to love.
Because it is in giving that we receive,
it is in forgiving that we are forgiven,
and it is in dying that we are born
to eternal life.

In the name of God, may every religion bring upon the earth
Justice and Peace, Forgiveness and Life, Love!

The words were said to be those of the Pope himself. There is a wistful sadness about the frail hope that they so emphatically hold up. We know it not to be so, yet we pray that it might yet be. The tomb of Francis was the place where this hope was so earnestly

expressed, and the photographs of these leaders of the world religions, against the familiar backdrop of that great basilica, went out around the world. It is hard to imagine a more appropriate site for such a gathering, or a more appropriate patron than St Francis.

In February 2003, just before the outbreak of the war in Iraq, Assisi was again the focus of international attention. The peace lamp was again lit and prayers were again offered.

Francis was invoked as the patron of inter faith dialogue and of peace. A key reason for this remains his own remarkable involvement in war and his own search for reconciliation. That simple tomb underneath the great basilica has become a world focus of prayer for peace.

ANYONE WHO DOES MANAGE TO FIND THE TIME to stay in Assisi is in for a treat. And it is a diverse, international and ecumenical treat. A place like St Anthony's Guesthouse for instance, is always filled with people from all over the world. The guests might be travelling students or large parish groups. They might be couples on the trip of a lifetime. They might be individuals from all sorts of religious backgrounds or of none in particular. They could be visiting their first great Christian shrine. Wherever they are from and whatever their religious or cultural background, many will find in Assisi a great gift. That gift is one of rediscovery – starting afresh with God and with the people of God. This really can happen in the broad and generous anonymity of such a wonderful place of pilgrimage.

How is this? One first important ecumenical fact is that Francis comes from way behind the troubles and religious battles of the more recent European centuries. Here is a major recognised holy person from our common undivided spiritual and intellectual past. The appeal of Francis to pilgrims of all backgrounds has to relate to the utter simplicity of what he said and did. He was always pointing directly to the life, example and teachings of Jesus. Here was an approach to life and to the world that seemed honest and uncontrived, across the generations and across the denominational divides.

Francis lived out Christian values that remain fresh and invigorating. This is what was so confronting about him, as well as being so very appealing. Priorities of life are what are at issue. Radical care for the needy, a deep desire for peace, utter respect for all creatures – all in the name of God. Francis appeals to a deep spiritual intuition; there is a fundamental satisfaction and overflowing grace that is to be found – difficult, sometimes very difficult and very often painful though this may be to live out. This is a basic Christian truth. It flows out of a love for God and a joyful recognition of God's love.

Somehow that shows in Assisi. You see it in the faces of those around you. You hear it in the responses to the mass. Whatever your mother tongue may be, the Latin or the Italian of the liturgy lives. A heart can thrill with the wonder of it all. It is across the cultures and across the religious traditions, in this most Italian and Catholic of places, that God is honoured. That is the truly ecumenical gift of Francis.

Dr John Davis is an Anglican parish priest in Melbourne, historian and former tertiary teacher. He first visited Assisi as a graduate student in 1972 – the first of many stays over the next 30 years with the American Sisters at St Anthony's Hospice. Arriving to admire the great 13th century art works, he also found the compelling and engaging presence of the Saint. His gratitude for the continuing Assisi experience is the underlying source of his enthusiasm for this way of coming to God.

Donald McMonigle is an Anglican priest currently working in aged care in Melbourne. A former Dean of Wangaratta Cathedral in rural Victoria, he was a parish priest for 20 years following several years of teaching prior to ordination. His long-standing association with Assisi and interest in Francis have been an ongoing source of inspiration. A visit this year to Franciscan sites in Cortona and Mount La Verna is the most recent of numerous pilgrimages made to Assisi and the Umbrian region.

Lynne Muir is an illustrator, calligrapher and book designer with a particular interest in Islamic and Celtic design. She received an Honour Award for her illustrations in the children's book, *Australian Owls, Frogmouths and Nightjars*. She designed and illustrated *The Gift of Saint Benedict*. After spending many years as a well-known folk singer, Lynne now enjoys singing classical music as an enthusiastic member of the Melbourne Chorale.

Cowan, James, *Francis: A Saint's Way*, Hodder and Stoughton, London, 2001.

Cunningham, Lawrence, *Saint Francis of Assisi*, Harper and Rowe, San Francisco, 1981.

Holland, Merlin and Hart-Davis, Rupert (eds.), *The Complete Letters of Oscar Wilde*, Henry Holt & Co, New York, 2000.

House, Adrian, *Francis of Assisi,* Pimlico, London, 2001.

Hudleston, Roger , Dom , *The Little Flowers of Saint Francis of Assisi*, The Heritage Press, New York.

Moorman, John R H, *Richest of Poor Men*, Darton Longman and Todd, London, 1977.

Robson, Michael, *St Francis of Assisi: The Legend and the Life*, Geoffrey Chapman, London, 1995.

Smith, John Holland, *Francis of Assisi*, Charles Scribner's Sons, New York, 1972.

PAX ET BONUM

By the door of just about every house in Assisi you may find a traditionally decorated ceramic tile. It might be blue or brown, or sometimes red. There are three words written on it – either in Italian or in Latin. Pax et bonum. Pace e bene. Peace and well-being. That is the greeting, the farewell or the blessing that comes to us from Francis. It is often used in everyday speech. Countless pilgrims and visitors take these tiles home from Assisi. They offer a continuing prayer, and are a visible sign of the gift of Francis.